A Mirrored Quilt

A Mirrored Quilt

Joanne Grumet

Clare Songbirds
Publishing House

Clare Songbirds Publishing House Poetry Series
ISBN 978-1-957221-29-8
Clare Songbirds Publishing House
A Mirrored Quilt © 2025 Joanne Grumet

Printed in the United States of America
FIRST EDITION

Cover art by Laura French created with Midjourney AI

140 Cottage Street
Auburn, New York 13021
www.claresongbirdspub.com

The author wishes to thank the publications in which these poems first appeared.

"lingua franca," in *BigCityLit.com* 2021

"Pokeweed," in *Garden of Eve,* (Finishing Line Press 2020)

"Lessons," in *One Art: A Journal of Poetry* November 28, 2021

"Florida," in *Jewish Women's Literary Annual* 2011

"At the Lecture," in *Jewish Women's Literary Annual* 2013

"Alzheimer's," previously published as "When Darkness Reached Out from under the Pine," in in *Garden of Eve* (Finishing Line Press 2020)

"Reflections," in *Write Launch* April 2023

"Ghosts of Second Ave," in *BigCityLit.Com 2022*

"In the Valley," in *Write Launch* April 2023

"Off the Bookshelf," in *The Bangalore Review 2021*

"In Tibet," in *Cathexis Northwest Press* March-April 2023

"A Mirrored Quilt" (the poem), a previous version appears in *Wisconsin Review 2021-2022*

Contents

lingua franca

my tongue is mute
servant of words

longs for pleasure
to lick at life

has tasted the sweet
and the bitter

Pokeweed

On a long stem
of pokeweed blooms
I grew, in Momma's
fragrant arms

Hard green berry,
I lived the summer
through, indifferent to
her sweet florets as

they fell. In autumn,
songbirds came
for my deep ripe fruit

and I learned to sing
the love she lavished
on me the summer through

Fox and Goose

One wintry afternoon
when I was four
I played Fox and Goose
in Emily's backyard with kids

from Beatrice Drive
We chased each other around
into safe spots
dug in the snow

Time and temperature
disappeared until
a warm liquid
ran down my legs

and when my leggings
turned to ice
I ran shivering home
to Momma

who toweled my red,
raw thighs and set me
in a warm tub to thaw

Ornithology

1.

What does a nice Jewish girl from Queens
know from birds? She knows from chickens.

Grandma Hannah Feigel's roasted chicken was the best, stuffed
with garlic, surrounded with meatballs of beef and veal.

We didn't visit much, but I still taste those meatballs
basted in garlicky chicken fat.

Momma told of Grandma Haya Hinda, raised in Belarus,
where the family shared their house

with the farm animals in winter. A chicken once jumped
on the dinner table and deposited an unwanted gift.

All the family laughed and laughed
except little Haya Hinda, who started to cry,

"If I had done that you would have really
spanked me!"

2.

What kind of bird does a Forest Hills
High School student learn about? Nightingales.

Not native to these shores, one flew from England
to New York on wings of Poesy,

singing in full-throated ease to my young, romantic soul
captivated by the beauty of Keats' language.

The poet's nightingale meant relief to him from existential pain, relief to me from boredom.

The bird arrived in folksongs as well, teaching me the ways of love from such lyrics as

The beautiful tale of the sweet nightingale
will never entice me to go...

She no more was afraid
to go down in the shade
for to hear the birds whistle and sing,
hear the birds whistle and sing.

3.
A spirit bird tops my totem pole
above the chicken and the nightingale,

discovered in my coffee grounds
by a kind woman

who flew here from Istanbul
to visit my friend Pinar's mother.

Its long wings spread out around
the inner rim of a small cup.

"This bird will protect you,"
she said.

Lessons

Henry, my father, was a sweet man,
had a smile for everyone.

He loved to sing opera
along with Jussi Bjorling

and the other tenors on the radio
though he didn't know the words.

When I was eighteen he gave me driving lessons
in our grey 1950s Buick Roadmaster.

One day, when we stopped for a light,
two young men in tee shirts

and slicked-back hair signaled my dad
to roll down the window.

"Your back wheels are going forward,"
they laughed.

My father laughed as well,
"All right boys," he said.

Later he said, "I had to answer them or
they might have called me dirty Jew."

I learned that day
how vulnerable he was,

how young men might
shame him for who he was

how his pain was my pain, too.

Strawberries

for your mouth,
Pa,
Kisses
for your wrinkled hands

Momma

It's been a long time
since I visited your
resting place next to Dad

My last words to you
in the hospital
were, "I'm going to be

a grandma."
Beneath all the plastic tubing
on your face,

you smiled

Florida

Troops of landscapers
slight and wiry
in their Day-Glo vests
fight back the looming growth
of scrubland.

They edge walkways of fancy residences,
trim hedges, harvest up the fallen leaves
from messy palms.

I recognize these young men as recent arrivals
to these swamplands
where melaleuca and pepper berry trees
have joined the native flora
and thrived,
although not always welcome.

They are more exposed to the sun
than transplants from the North:
the Canadians, Vermonters and New Yorkers
who survive inside, in air-conditioned niches.

I do not know them, have only smiled hello,
but they remind me of the slender youths
who dug my mother's grave down here
in the sandy soil.

I wanted so much to speak with them—
her final caretakers—
as they waited quietly for the last mourner,
a lingering daughter,
to leave them to their work.

Goodbye

We packed you in the Volvo
for your long trip home.
Sweet to see you and the kiddies
wrenching to watch you go.

Later, in the wash, tumbling
from the dryer, amid
the worn dish towels, the not-
quite- white underwear, a dark
blue shirt and a pair of grey
long johns, I found
one bright pink and white
Hello Kitty sock
labeled "Wednesday."

Legacy

Your great-great- grandparents,
 Jacob, Anna,
had an inn near Vitebsk
where the Czar's postmen changed horses.

They bundled up the family
and Anna wrapped the Sabbath candlesticks
in her feather bed as they hurried to leave.

Brass candlesticks, one slightly bent
from when a drunken Cossack
tossed it to the floor.

Brass candlesticks my mother lit,
the very ones I light on Shabbos when you,
my beloved ones, come to visit.

They are weighted with pride, tradition,
grief and shame
but there is transcendence
in the weightless flames.

At the Lecture

The young scholar spoke
about his trip to Romania
seeking the roots of klezmer music there
He found them in the villages of
Hungarians, Romanians, and Gypsies
but few fruits

Few there knew the music of the
Jewish villages
Only the Roma, souls who once had played
at Jewish weddings,
remembered

"How can you talk about this music," complained a man,
perhaps a survivor,
"without mentioning the Iron Guard and the slaughter of the Jews,
surpassing the Nazis
in brutality?"

"I could not have that mindset,"
replied the speaker
"and hope to connect, but when I played
the music there
everyone was moved"

Then the young scholar took out his violin
and played for us

And we danced

Alzheimer's

When darkness reached out from under the pine
and the path was hidden away in fright
I lost my footing in tangled vines
The grass that June was perfumed with thyme
but something that day was not quite right
and darkness reached out from under the pine.

Slowing his steps he sat for a time
and when I saw him in his plight
I lost my footing in tangled vines.

Nothing to do but stop our climb
as the frogs jumped away in fright
and darkness reached out from under the pine.

In the forest of grief I missed the signs
how to manage in day-turned -to -night
and I lost my footing in tangled vines

When the moan of the mourning dove combined
with the flap of her wings in frenzied flight
when darkness reached out from under the pine
I lost my footing in tangled vines.

August Angst

Frogs sing in the pond
down the hill
as he pays late credit card bills
in the kitchen

Dates go by without note
and debts go by without payment—
his memory worse—
a tremor in our foundation

Out here on the porch
flies buzz round my head,
wild roses scent the air,
and the dog snoozes

Down the hill,
frogs sing in the pond

Here

I don't have time this Halloween
for kids in costumes at the door
or spirits of the dead floating around
unmoored,

not even for our departed friend
if he returns to visit in my dreams again
playing hide and seek, smiling,
as if to say "Yes, I'm really here."

Really here? What does that mean?
I don't have time for such questions
or for the play of boisterous children.

I only have the wherewithal
to get you through the long night,
making sure you are still really here.

Mount Hebron Cemetery

They will let me rest
 a woman near her man
against Orthodox tradition

What could we possibly do
under those dark covers
in that long, long night?

LOVE IS ETERNAL

we wrote on the stone

DEAREST HUSBAND
FATHER
GRANDFATHER

we wrote

A GOOD SOUL

What will the children write on mine?
Will they find comfort in choosing the right words,
in holding each other as they mourn?

Will they forgive each other their hurts
from long ago or more recent slights?
Will they forgive me?

A New Suitor

Although I will not stop for him,
he follows me

He stood by my beloved's bed
in turned-up soil, smiling

Now in the mirror
by my bed

I see him reaching out
as I turn away

Intimacy

"Intimacy and longing for intimacy, one song" ~Rumi

A man and woman
lived together
many years

in harmony.
When the man died
his widow

mourned him deeply.
She told neighbors
of her grief; they felt her sorrow.

One remarked
how lucky she was;
he had no one

whose loss
would cause him
such pain.

Letting Go

Our boots thump across
the wooden bridge
in the woods no more

If I find its handrail
in my dreams,
should I hold on

or balance myself
on emptiness?

Early March

1.
Leaves chewed up, spit out
by winter
mulch the pale, dead grass,
soggy from the thaw

Twigs and branches
like broken bones
litter the field, remnants
of battles with wind and ice

Denuded sycamores
expose their peeling skin
their scars.
Everywhere is brown

2.
I climb down a hole
in the thawing earth,
crawl the tangled roots
of a friendly tree
and float up the trunk
on rising sap

Reflections

I wake to view myself
through the window
robed in flimsy summer clouds
my sky-blue complexion
unblemished

I wash my face in the nearby stream,
a watery mirror,
window to a time
before words
before memory

Ghosts of Second Avenue

i.

We courted in a world that is no more:
the Gem Spa where we went
for chocolate egg creams; Ratner's Dairy Restaurant
where they served us onion rolls for bread;
the Second Avenue Deli

No more readings by the Beats,
Ginsberg gone, his howling;
no more Fugs protesting
the war in Vietnam,
the Fillmore East come and gone

ii.

Scotty's studio apartment
on the tenth floor
overlooked St. Mark's Churchyard

We slept on a mattress
on the floor,
in each other's arms

I told him of the abortion I had
before we met

He said nothing
Was he already asleep?

Now he sleeps. He sleeps,
I'll never know

Sitting in that churchyard,
among the spirits of long-gone Dutch

settlers, I hear his voice, "Enjoy.
Enjoy your happiness," it says

A New Love

He will pick me up at 10 a.m.
on Wednesday

and we will drive out
to the beach

We might kiss hello
in the car

and dance around our fears:
Is this feeling real?

How soon before we
grab each other?

This Morning

A yahrzeit candle
for my husband
has almost finished burning

I move it next to the orchid
you gave me,

 a present for our
one-year-since-we-met
anniversary

a flame, a flower

In the Valley

I walk north where garlic mustard grows
with heart-shaped leaves,
clusters of tiny white stars.

Their slender stalks border a trail
into the woods
past a brook where the deer drink.

Back in Manhattan
they nod to me
on my solitary walks

along the river,
reminding me of the path
to your house.

I flow like the Hudson,
Mohicanituck in Lenape,
river that moves in both directions.

Off the Bookshelf

The Essence of T'AI CHI CH'UAN The Literary Tradition
(Translated and ed. by Benjamin Pang Jeng Lo et alia)

My copy is falling apart;
frontispiece with Chinese writing,
Preface, Introduction no longer
attached to the spine.

The soul of the book survives,
in calligraphy and ageless wisdom.
"Be still as a mountain," wrote Wu Yu-hsiang.
"Move like a great river."

"Move like a cat," he wrote,
but when I gently turn a page to read,
it detaches. "In discontinuity," he wrote,
"there is still continuity."

In Tibet

sculpted Ice Buddha
melts in the Kyichu River
water to water

A Mirrored Quilt

The past is pieced together
 from shards of looking glass
with edges smoothed
from years of use, yet
sometimes on a jagged edge,
I cut myself.

Photograph courtesy of Kearsten Leder

Joanne Grumet has always been in love with language and worked as a lexicographer and later taught Linguistics and Writing to Non-native Speakers. Her chapbook *Garden of Eve* was published in 2020 and her poems can be found in journals and anthologies in The United States, India, and Israel. In addition, her poetry can be found in the archives of the Brooklyn Museum and her poetry and songs were featured on cable tv in South Deerfield, Massachusetts.